초등 영어독해를 쉽고 재미있게!

# 똑똑한 초등영어독해 jump❶ [개정판]

초등 영어독해를 쉽고 재미있게!

# 똑똑한 초등영어독해 jump ❶ [개정판]

2007년 11월 06일  초판  1쇄 발행
2024년   4월 17일  개정  1쇄 인쇄
2024년   4월 25일  개정  1쇄 발행

**지은이** 국제어학연구소 영어학부
**감수** Jenny Kim
**그림** 조한유
**펴낸이** 이규인
**펴낸곳** 국제어학연구소 출판부

**출판등록** 2010년 1월 18일 제302-2010-000006호
**주소** 서울특별시 마포구 대흥로4길 49, 1층(용강동 월명빌딩)
**Tel** (02) 704-0900 **팩시밀리** (02) 703-5117
**홈페이지** www.bookcamp.co.kr
**e-mail** changbook1@hanmail.net
**ISBN** 979-11-9875870-5  13740
**정가** 13,000원

영어의 기초를 다져 주는
# magic 시리즈

초등 영어독해를 쉽고 재미있게!

# 똑똑한 초등 영어독해

## Jump ①
[개정판]

글 국제어학연구소 영어학부 | **감수** Jenny Kim | **그림** 조한유

ILR 국제어학연구소

# 머리말

언어를 익히는 것에 있어서 책을 많이 있는 것처럼 중요한 것은 없습니다. 문화, 사회, 과학, 예술 등 여러 분야의 책을 읽으면 자신의 지식을 넓힐 수 있고, 언어를 사용함에 있어서도 풍부한 에너지를 키울 수 있습니다. 영어를 배우는 과정에서도 이러한 과정은 필요합니다. 긴 내용의 책을 한 권씩 읽는 것도 좋지만, 짧은 내용의 지문을 읽으면서 영어의 지식을 넓히는 것도 매우 도움이 됩니다.

이 책은 아이들이 여러 분야의 내용들을 짧은 지문을 통해서 읽어보는 것에 중점을 두었습니다. 또한 자신이 읽은 내용이 어떤 내용인지 스스로 생각하여 문제를 풀어보고, 그 지문에 나온 단어들을 익히도록 구성하였습니다. 천천히 한 단원씩 읽어 나가면서 글의 내용을 자신의 지식으로 만들 수 있기를 바랍니다.

영어를 학습함에 있어서는 자기 스스로 하려는 자세가 매우 중요합니다. 자기 수준에 적합한 책을 선정하여 듣고, 읽고, 생각하는 것을 반복하여 자신의 영어 지식으로 만들어야 합니다. 그래서 이 교재는 단계별로 구성하였습니다. 자신의 수준에 알맞은 것을 골라서 스스로 학습하는 자세를 키워나가기를 바랍니다.

# 이 책의 구성

 **Before Reading**

스토리에 대한 이해도를 높이기 위하여 새로운 단어와 중요 표현을 미리 익혀요.

 **Story**

앞에서 배운 단어와 표현을 생각하면서 스토리를 이해해요.

 **Vocabulary**

배운 단어들을 2가지 형태의 쓰기 문제를 통해 확인해요.

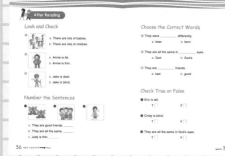

 **After Reading**

스토리를 얼마나 이해했는지 자신의 실력을 체크해 봐요.

 **Story Comprehension**

스토리에 대한 이해도를 종합적으로 확인해 봐요.

# 차례

**Before Reading**

## New Words

piglet

in

mud

lamb

by

on

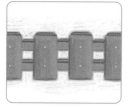

fence

calf

behind

## Key Expression

Tom is under the fence.

❶ Tom is ___ by ___ the fence. (by)

❷ Tom is _____ the fence. (behind)

# Where is the piglet?

There are baby animals in the farm.

Where is the piglet?

It is in the mud.

Where is the lamb?

It is by the mud.

Where is the duckling?

It is on the fence.

Where is the calf?

It is behind the fence.

## Vocabulary

# Write the Words

| in | calf | fence | piglet | by | lamb |

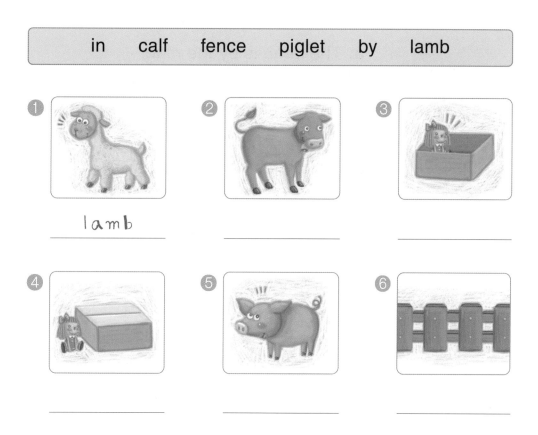

① lamb

②

③

④

⑤

⑥

# Unscramble the Letters

① 
d

m u

mud

② 
e i d

b h n

## After Reading

# Look and Check

a. The lamb is by the mud.

b. The duckling is by the mud.

a. The calf is behind the fence.

b. The calf is in front of the fence.

a. The piglet is in the mud.

b. The piglet is by the mud.

# Number the Sentences

a. The doll is on the box. ___3___

b. The doll is by the box. _____

c. The doll is in the box. _____

# Choose the Correct Words

1. The piglet is _____ the mud.

    a. on                    b. in

2. The lamb is _____ the mud.

    a. in                    b. by

3. The duckling is _____ the fence.

    a. on                    b. under

# Check True or False

1. There are baby animals in the farm.

    T ☐                    F ☐

2. The piglet is on the fence.

    T ☐                    F ☐

3. The duckling is between the fence.

    T ☐                    F ☐

## Story Comprehension

1 What's the main idea?

  a. The fence

  b. Babies in the house

  c. Baby animals of the farm

2 Where is the piglet?

  a. It is in the mud.

  b. It is on the fence.

  c. It is under the fence.

3 Where is the duckling?

  a. It is by the mud.

  b. It is on the fence.

  c. It is behind the fence.

4 Which animal is by the mud?

  a. lamb        b. piglet        c. duckling

5 Which animal is behind the fence?

  a. dog        b. calf        c. duckling

## Before Reading

## New Words

younger

naughty

break

vase

throw

book

pull

tail

## Key Expression

Don't **do that, Jim.**

1. _____ run here, Kate.

2. _____ make a noise, Sam.

# Don't do that, Jim.

I have a younger brother.

His name is Jim.

He is a naughty boy.

He breaks one of the vases.

My mom says, "Don't do that, Jim."

He throws the books.

My dad says, "Don't do that, Jim."

He pulls the dog's tail.

My family says to him, "Don't do that, Jim."

## Vocabulary

# Write the Words

| throw | book | naughty | younger | pull | tail |

① _____

② _____

③ _____

④ _____

⑤ _____

⑥ _____

# Unscramble the Letters

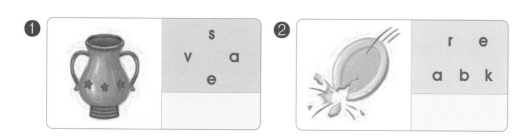

① s v a e

② r e a b k

# After Reading

## Look and Check

a. He breaks one of the vases.

b. He touches one of the vases.

a. He throws the balls.

b. He throws the books.

a. He pulls the dog's tail.

b. He touches the dog's nose.

## Number the Sentences

a. My mom says, "Don't do that." _____

b. I have a younger brother. _____

c. He is a naughty boy. _____

# Choose the Correct Words

① My brother's name is _____.

    a. Jim          b. Sally

② My dad _____, "Don't do that, Jim."

    a. say          b. says

③ _____ pulls the dog's tail.

    a. We          b. He

# Check True or False

❶ I have an older brother.

    T ☐          F ☐

❷ He is a shy boy.

    T ☐          F ☐

❸ He breaks one of the vases.

    T ☐          F ☐

## Story Comprehension

① What's the main idea?

    a. My dog's tail

    b. My mom and dad

    c. My younger brother

② The girl's brother is _____.

    a. kind          b. cute          c. naughty

③ What's the younger brother's name? _____

④ What does her family say to her brother?

    a. Good boy!

    b. Not now!

    c. Don't do that!

⑤ What is not true?

    a. He reads a book.

    b. He breaks the vase.

    c. He pulls the dog's tail.

## Before Reading

# New Words

mice

hungry

sleepy

food

climb

stairs

find

cheese

# Key Expression

They are looking for food.

① I _____ _____ _____ my toys.

② She _____ _____ _____ the jacket.

# The three mice

There are three mice.

The three mice are hungry.

They are sleepy, too.

They are looking for food.

They are climbing the stairs.

Finally, they find cheese on the third floor.

And three beds are there, too.

They eat the cheese.

They are full now.

The three mice want to go to bed now.

# Vocabulary

## Write the Words

| hungry | mice | climb | stairs | find | cheese |

 ①

 ②

 ③

 ④

 ⑤

 ⑥

## Unscramble the Letters

**1**
y e
p l
s e

**2**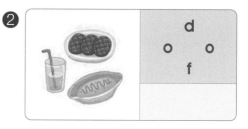
d
o o
f

## After Reading

## Look and Check

a. There are three cats.
b. There are three mice.

a. Three mice are walking the stairs.
b. Three mice are climbing the stairs.

a. Three mice want to go to bed.
b. Three mice want to go to house.

## Number the Sentences

a. There are three beds. _____

b. The three mice are full. _____

c. The three mice are hungry. _____

# Choose the Correct Words

1 Three mice are hungry and _____.

    a. full                b. sleepy

2 There are cheese on the third _____.

    b. box               b. floor

3 Three _____ want to go to bed.

    a. mouse            b. mice

# Check True or False

1 The three mice are climbing up the tree.

    T ☐              F ☐

2 They find cheese on the second floor.

    T ☐              F ☐

3 The three mice eat the cheese.

    T ☐              F ☐

# Story Comprehension

1 What's the main idea?

   a. Three small mice

   b. Three happy mice

   c. Three hungry mice

2 What are the three mice looking for?

   a. food          b. beds          c. stairs

3 Where are they climbing?

   a. roof          b. table         c. stairs

4 Where do the three mice find cheese?

   a. the first floor

   b. the second floor

   c. the third floor

5 What do they want to after eating?

   a. They want to eat more.

   b. They want to drink something.

   c. They want to go to bed.

## Before Reading

# New Words

run

jump

sing

study

teacher

play

friend

# Key Expression

I learn to **sing from the birds.**

❶ We _____ _____ skate.

❷ They _____ _____ play the piano.

## Story

# I learn many things.

I learn many things from animals.

I learn to run from a dog.

I learn to jump from a cat.

I learn to sing from a bird.

I am happy with animals.

And I learn many things from people.

I learn to read books from my dad.

I learn to study from my teacher.

I learn to play from my friends.

I am happy with people.

## Vocabulary

## Write the Words

| jump | run | study | teacher | sing |

_____ _____ _____

_____ _____

## Unscramble the Letters

e
d i
f r n

p
y l
a

## After Reading

## Look and Check

a. I learn to sing from a dog.
b. I learn to sing from a bird.

a. I learn to jump from a cat.
b. I learn to jump from my mom.

a. I learn to study from animals.
b. I learn to study from my teacher.

## Number the Sentences

a. I learn to read books from my dad. _____

b. I learn to play from my friends. _____

c. I learn to run from a dog. _____

# Choose the Correct Words

1 I learn to _____ from my friends.

    a. play              b. sing

2 I learn to read books from _____.

    a. a cat              b. my dad

3 I learn to study from my _____.

    a. people            b. teacher

# Check True or False

1 I learn to sing from a bird.

    T ☐              F ☐

2 I learn to run from my friends.

    T ☐              F ☐

3 I learn many things from people.

    T ☐              F ☐

## Story Comprehension

① What's the main idea?

    a. My friends

    b. Learning many things

    c. Studying many things

② What does the girl learn from a dog?

    a. running        b. jumping        c. singing

③ What does the girl learn from her teacher?

    a. reading        b. studying        c. playing

④ What does the girl learn from her friends?

    a. walking        b. running        c. playing

⑤ What is not true?

    a. The girl learns to sing from a bird.

    b. The girl feels happy with the animals.

    c. The girl feels sad with the people.

## Before Reading

## New Words

children

fat

thin

short

tall

deaf

blind

same

## Key Expression

**They** were born **differently.**

❶ I ＿＿＿＿＿ ＿＿＿＿＿ in 1995.

❷ The puppies ＿＿＿＿＿ ＿＿＿＿＿ last year.

# They are good friends.

There are a lot of children.

Judy is thin.

Jake is blind.

Annie is fat.

Cindy is deaf.

Eric is tall.

Peter is short.

They were born differently.

They are all the same in God's eyes.

They are good friends.

## Vocabulary

# Write the Words

| fat | blind | same | tall | thin | short |

①

② 

③ 

④ 

⑤ 

⑥ 

_____   _____   _____

_____   _____   _____

# Unscramble the Letters

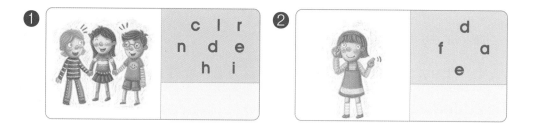

① c l r
n d e
h i

② d
f a
e

## After Reading

# Look and Check

a. There are lots of babies.

b. There are lots of children.

a. Annie is fat.

b. Annie is thin.

a. Jake is deaf.

b. Jake is blind.

# Number the Sentences

❶   ❷   ❸

a. They are good friends. _____

b. They are all the same. _____

c. Judy is thin. _____

# Choose the Correct Words

① They were _____ differently.

      a. bear            b. born

② They are all the same in _____ eyes.

      a. God            b. God's

③ They are _____ friends.

      a. bad            b. good

# Check True or False

❶ Eric is tall.

      T ☐            F ☐

❷ Cindy is blind.

      T ☐            F ☐

❸ They are all the same in God's eyes.

      T ☐            F ☐

## Story Comprehension

1 What's the main idea?

   a. God's eyes

   b. A little difference in children

   c. Children's different character

2 Who is tall?   _____

3 Who is deaf?   _____

4 Who is short?   _____

5 Who is blind?   _____

## Before Reading

# New Words

new

cradle

clothes

clean

living room

bathtub

teddy bear

robot

# Key Expression

Dad is making a cradle.

① I _____ _____ the room. (clean)

② They _____ _____ cards. (play)

# When will the baby come?

We will have a new baby.

Dad is making a cradle.

Mom is making baby's clothes.

My sister is cleaning the living room.

I'm cleaning the baby's bathtub.

"When will the baby come?" I ask mom.

Mom says, "Soon."

I will give my teddy bear to the baby.

I will give my robot to the baby.

# Vocabulary

## Write the Words

| clean | bathtub | teddy bear | living room | clothes | new |

①

②

③

④

⑤

⑥

## Unscramble the Letters

❶

r d e
c l
a

❷

b o t
r o

## After Reading

# Look and Check

a. Mom is making shoes.

b. Mom is making clothes.

a. Sister is cleaning the bathroom.

b. Sister is cleaning the living room.

a. Dad is making a chair.

b. Dad is making a cradle.

# Number the Sentences

a. I am cleaning the bathtub. _____

b. We will have a new baby. _____

c. I will give my robot. _____

# Choose the Correct Words

**1** When will the baby _____?

      a. came         b. come

**2** I will give my teddy bear _____.

      a. the baby         b. to the baby

**3** We will have a _____ baby.

      a. new         b. old

# Check True or False

**1** I will give my books to the baby.

      T ☐         F ☐

**2** Dad is making a little house.

      T ☐         F ☐

**3** My sister is cleaning the living room.

      T ☐         F ☐

# Story Comprehension

1. What's the main idea?

   a. My family

   b. Cleaning the house

   c. Waiting a new baby

2. Who is making a cradle?

   a. Dad          b. Mom          c. my brother

3. Who is cleaning the living room?

   a. Dad          b. Mom          c. my sister

4. What is Mom making for baby?

   a. hat          b. pants          c. clothes

5. What will the boy give to the baby?

   a. a book and pencils

   b. the clothes and shoes

   c. a teddy bear and a robot

## Before Reading

## New Words

hen

duck

egg

hatch

little

chick

duckling

walk

## Key Expression

The hen's baby is chick.

1 The _____ baby is puppy. (dog)

2 The _____ baby is duckling. (duck)

**Story**

# They are so cute!

There are a hen and a duck.

The hen sits on her egg.

The duck sits on her egg, too.

The hen's egg hatches.

The duck's egg hatches, too.

The hen says, "My little chick!"

The duck says, "My little duckling!"

The chick and the duckling are walking.

They are so cute!

## Vocabulary

# Write the Words

| egg | duck | hatch | hen | chick | duckling |
| --- | --- | --- | --- | --- | --- |

①

②

③

④

⑤

⑥

# Unscramble the Letters

①

l t t
i e
l

②

w k
a l

## After Reading

# Look and Check

a. There are a hen and a duck.

b. There are hens and ducks.

a. The duck sits on her egg.

b. The duck stands on her egg.

a. The duckling is walking.

b. The duckling is running.

# Number the Sentences

a. The hen's egg hatches. _____

b. They are so cute. _____

c. They are walking. _____

# Choose the Correct Words

1 The hen sits _____ her egg.

    a. on                     b. up

2 The _____ egg hatches.

    a. ducks               b. duck's

3 The chick and duckling are so _____.

    a. big                b. cute

# Check True or False

1 The duck says, "My little duckling."

    T ☐                 F ☐

2 The hen's baby is duckling.

    T ☐                 F ☐

3 The chick and duckling are flying.

    T ☐                 F ☐

## Story Comprehension

1. What's the main idea?

   a. Animals

   b. A hen and her chick

   c. A chick and a duckling

2. What is hen's baby called ?

   a. chick          b. puppy          c. duckling

3. What is duck's baby called ?

   a. chick          b. puppy          c. duckling

4. What do the chick and the duckling do?

   a. They are eating.

   b. They are singing.

   c. They are walking.

5. What is not true?

   a. The hen sits on her chick.

   b. The hen says, "My little chick."

   c. The chick and the duckling are so cute.

## Before Reading

# New Words

like

grandma

grandpa

hate

pinch

arm

scold

angry

sad

# Key Expression

Mom and Dad liked me. (I)

1 Sam liked _____. (she)

2 Judy liked _____. (he)

## Story

# I am very sad.

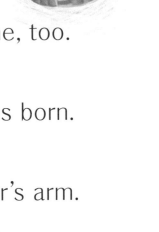

My family all liked me.

Mom and Dad liked me.

Grandma and Grandpa liked me, too.

Nobody likes me anymore,

because my younger sister was born.

I hate my sister.

So I pinched my younger sister's arm.

Mom and Dad are angry at me.

Grandma and Grandpa scold me.

I am very sad.

# Vocabulary

## Write the Words

| grandma | arm | pinch | grandpa | sad | like |
|---------|-----|-------|---------|-----|------|

①

②

③

④

⑤

⑥

## Unscramble the Letters

①

a　t
h　e

②

s　l　d
c　o

## After Reading

# Look and Check

a. The puppy was born.

b. My younger sister was born .

a. I was sad.

b. I was angry.

a. Mom and Dad liked me.

b. Mom and Dad hated me.

# Number the Sentences

a. Grandma liked me. _____

b. I was very sad. _____

c. I hate my sister. _____

# Choose the Correct Words

1. My family all liked _____.

   a. me          b. my

2. Nobody likes me _____.

   a. more          b. anymore

3. My younger sister _____ born.

   a. was          b. were

# Check True or False

1. Mom and Dad liked me.

   T ☐          F ☐

2. My younger brother was born.

   T ☐          F ☐

3. Grandma and Grandpa scolded me.

   T ☐          F ☐

# Story Comprehension

**1** What's the main idea?

   a. My younger sister

   b. I like my younger sister.

   c. Nobody likes me anymore.

**2** My _____ sister was born.

   a. older           b. younger       c. pretty

**3** Why does the boy hate his sister?

   a. Because nobody likes him anymore.

   b. Because everybody hates his sister.

   c. Because everybody hates his Dad.

**4** What did the boy do to his sister?

   a. He hugged his sister.

   b. He pinched his sister.

   c. He played with his sister.

**5** What is not true?

   a. Mom and Dad were angry at the boy.

   b. Grandma and Grandpa scolded the boy.

   c. The boy is very happy.

## Before Reading

## New Words

hippo

doctor

sick

stomachache

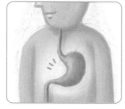

stomach

take out

car

truck

boat

## Key Expression

I have a stomachache.

❶ She _____ a _____ . (headache)

❷ I _____ a _____ . (toothache)

**Story**

## Toys in Baby Hippo's stomach

Mommy Hippo says,

"Doctor, doctor, my baby is sick."

Doctor says, "What's the matter?"

Baby Hippo says, "I have a stomachache."

Doctor says, "Let me see...

Ah, there are toys in your stomach."

Doctor takes out the toys.

A car, a truck, and a boat!

Doctor says, "Are you okay, now?"

Baby Hippo says,

"I feel much better. Thank you, Doctor."

## Vocabulary

## Write the Words

| boat | doctor | truck | stomachache | car | hippo |

1

2

3

4

5

6

## Unscramble the Letters

1

2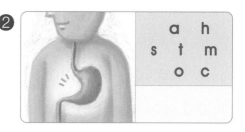

# Look and Check

a. Baby hippo has a headache.

b. Baby hippo has a stomachache.

a. Baby Hippo says, "I'm sorry, Doctor."

b. Baby Hippo says, "Thank you, Doctor."

a. There are toys in your stomach.

b. There are fruits in your stomach.

# Number the Sentences

a. I have a stomachache. _____

b. Are you okay, now? _____

c. I feel much better. _____

# Choose the Correct Words

1 My baby is _____.

    a. sick               b. sleepy

2 _____'s the matter?

    a. Why              b. What

3 I feel _____ better.

    a. many            b. much

# Check True or False

1 Baby Hippo has a headache.

    T ☐             F ☐

2 There are toys in Baby Hippo's stomach.

    T ☐             F ☐

3 The Baby Hippo feels much better.

    T ☐             F ☐

## Story Comprehension

1  What's the main idea?

 a. Doctor and Baby Hippo

 b. Baby Hippo's stomachache

 c. Mommy Hippo and Baby Hippo

2  What's wrong with Baby Hippo?

 a. He has a headache.

 b. He has a toothache.

 c. He has a stomachache.

3  What are Baby Hippo's stomach in?

 a. toys          b. food          c. coins

4  Who took the toys out in Baby Hippo's stomach?

 a. Doctor          b. Baby Hippo          c. Mommy Hippo

5  Why Baby hippo was sick?

 a. Because he ate his toys.

 b. Because he ran too much.

 c. Because he ate ice cream.

## Before Reading

### New Words

pretty

girl

shy

bite

nail

pick

nose

## Key Expression

> She often bites her nails.

1 She _____ picks her nose. (sometimes)

2 Cindy _____ bites her nails. (never)

 **Story**

## Cindy's bad habits

Cindy is a pretty girl.

She is a shy girl.

She has bad habits.

She often bites her nails.

She sometimes picks her nose.

Whenever she bites her nails,

Mom says, "Don't do that!"

When she picks her nose,

Dad says, "Don't do that!"

Now, Cindy never bites her nails.

She never picks her nose.

# Vocabulary

## Write the Words

| pretty | nail | girl | bite | nose |
|--------|------|------|------|------|

①

②

③

_____

④

⑤

_____

## Unscramble the Letters

❶

c i k p

❷

y h s

## After Reading

# Look and Check

a. She bites her arm.

b. She bites her nails.

a. She picks her nose.

b. She picks her mouth.

a. Good morning!

b. Don't do that!

# Number the Sentences

a. She is a shy girl. _____

b. She bites her nails. _____

c. She is a pretty girl. _____

# Choose the Correct Words

1 Cindy had bad _____.

      a. hands             b. habits

2 She often _____ her nails.

      a. bite              b. bites

3 Her father said, "_____ do that!"

      a. Doesn't          b. Don't

# Check True or False

1 Cindy is a bad girl.

      T ☐            F ☐

2 Cindy had good habits.

      T ☐            F ☐

3 Cindy often bites her nails.

      T ☐            F ☐

## Story Comprehension

1 What's the main idea?

   a. A shy girl     b. Cindy's family     c. Cindy's habits

2 What is not Cindy's habits?

   a. Biting her nails.

   b. Picking her nose.

   c. Scratching her head.

3 What did her parents say to Cindy?

   a. Don't by shy.    b. Don't do that.    c. Don't be late.

4 How can Cindy fix her habits?

   a. Thanks to her parents

   b. Thanks to her friends

   c. Thanks to her teacher

5 What is not true?

   a. Cindy is a pretty girl.

   b. Cindy has bad habits.

   c. Cindy still bites her nails.

## Before Reading

## New Words

hot

summer

water

woods

fox

thirsty

meet

crow

## Key Expression

**Where** are **you** going?

❶ What _____ they _____? (do)

❷ Where _____ he _____? (go)

# May I go with you?

It is a hot summer day.

There is no water in the woods.

The fox is thirsty.

So he leaves the woods to look for water.

The fox meets the crow on his way.

The crow says to the fox,

"Where are you going?"

The fox says, "I'm going to look for water."

"May I go with you?" says the crow.

"Sure!" says the fox.

So they go to look for water together.

# Vocabulary

## Write the Words

| thirsty | fox | woods | hot | summer | crow |

①

②

③

④

⑤

⑥

## Unscramble the Letters

❶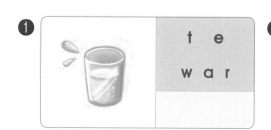

t  e
w  a  r

❷

t
m  e
e

# Look and Check

①

   a. There is no water in the woods.

   b. There is no trees in the woods.

②

   a. The fox is thirsty.

   b. The fox is hungry.

③

   a. The fox meets the crow.

   b. The cat meets the crow.

# Number the Sentences

①     ②     ③

a. Where are you going? _____

b. It is a hot summer day. _____

c. "Sure," says the fox. _____

# Choose the Correct Words

1 Where are you _____?

    a. go               b. going

2 May I go _____ you?

    a. and            b. with

3 There _____ no water in the woods.

    a. is              b. are

# Check True or False

1 It is a rainy summer day.

    T ☐           F ☐

2 There is lots of water in the woods.

    T ☐           F ☐

3 The fox and the crow go to look for water.

    T ☐           F ☐

## Story Comprehension

1. What's the main idea?

   a. Animals　　　　b. The woods　　　c. Finding water

2. It is a _____ summer day.

   a. warm　　　　　b. hot　　　　　　c. cold

3. Where does the fox live?

   a. in the city

   b. in the farm

   c. in the woods

4. The fox meets the _____ on his way.

   a. boy　　　　　　b. cow　　　　　　c. crow

5. What does the crow say to the fox?

   a. May I go with you?

   b. May I eat your food?

   c. May I drink your water?

## Before Reading

# New Words

cook

chef

sandwiches

hot dog

hot cakes

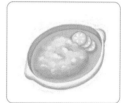

scrambled egg

delicious

cake

# Key Expression

Judy is good at cooking.

1 I _____ _____ _____ singing.

2 They _____ _____ _____ dancing.

 **Story**

## Judy loves cooking.

People loves to eat.

But Judy loves cooking.

She is good at cooking.

So she wants to be a good chef.

Sometimes she made food for her family.

She made sandwiches for Mom.

She made a hot dog for Dad.

She made hot cakes for her brother.

She made a scrambled egg for herself.

They were all delicious.

Next time, Judy will try to bake a cake.

## Vocabulary

# Write the Words

scrambled egg  cake  hot dog  hot cakes  sandwiches  cook

①

②

③

_____    _____    _____

④

⑤

⑥

_____    _____    _____

# Unscramble the Letters

①

e c f h

②

d i u c s e i l o

## After Reading

# Look and Check

a. Judy loves eating.

b. Judy loves cooking.

a. She made sandwiches for Mom.

b. She made sandwiches with Mom.

a. She made a hot dog for Dad.

b. She made hot cakes for Dad.

# Number the Sentences

a. She wants to be a good chef. _____

b. People loves to eat. _____

c. She made a scrambled egg. _____

## Choose the Correct Words

1 Judy is _____ at cooking.

    a. well              b. good

2 She made _____ for her brother.

    a. a doll           b. hot cakes

3 Judy made a scrambled egg for _____.

    a. herself          b. himself

## Check True or False

1 Judy made a scrambled egg for herself.

    T ☐           F ☐

2 The foods were very delicious.

    T ☐           F ☐

3 Judy's dream is to be a doctor.

    T ☐           F ☐

## Story Comprehension

1 What's the main idea?

    a. Eating        b. Cooking        c. Helping

2 Who made the foods for family?

    a. Dad        b. Brother        c. Judy

3 What does Judy like to do?

    a. watching TV

    b. playing the ball

    c. cooking the foods

4 What did Judy make for Dad?

    a. sandwiches

    b. a hot dog

    c. a scrambled egg

5 The foods were _____.

    a. terrible        b. not good        c. delicious

## Before Reading

## New Words

high chair

blue

sit

eat

say

paint

pink

think

## Key Expression

Let's paint the high chair pink.

❶ _____ play together.

❷ _____ go home now.

# Jake had a high chair.

Jake had a high chair.

The chair was blue.

He sat on it and ate food.

One day, his dad said to him,

"Let's paint the high chair pink."

Jake asked, "Why, Dad?"

Dad said, "For your younger sister."

Jake thought and said, "Okay, Dad."

They painted it pink.

## Vocabulary

# Write the Words

| paint | say | high chair | eat | pink | blue |

# Unscramble the Letters

t
i s

t k
h i n

## After Reading

## Look and Check

a. Jake had a arm chair.

b. Jake had a high chair.

a. The chair is blue.

b. The chair is brown.

a. He sat on it and played.

b. He sat on it and ate food.

## Number the Sentences

a. He ate food with his family. _____

b. He sat on the high chair. _____

c. They painted the high chair pink. _____

# Choose the Correct Words

1 Let's _____ the high chair pink.

    a. make                b. paint

2 Jake _____ and said, "Okay, Dad."

    a. thinks             b. thought

3 He sat on it and _____ food with his family.

    a. eat               b. ate

# Check True or False

1 Jack's high chair was blue.

    T ☐            F ☐

2 Jake's sister had a high chair, too.

    T ☐            F ☐

3 They painted the high chair yellow.

    T ☐            F ☐

## Story Comprehension

1 What's the main idea?

   a. Jake's dad

   b. Jake's sister

   c. The high chair

2 What color was Jake's high chair?

   a. pink         b. blue         c. green

3 Jake thought and said, "_____, Dad."

   a. Okay        b. Oh, no       c. Sorry

4 For whom did they paint?

   a. Jake's sister

   b. Jake's brother

   c. Jake's friend

5 What color is the high chair now?

   a. pink         b. blue         c. yellow

## Before Reading

## New Words

sunny

go

picnic

this

lost

kitten

give

meal

name

## Key Expression

My family **went on** a picnic.

❶ I _____ _____ a visit.

❷ We _____ _____ a trip.

**Story**

# We named him Kitty.

It was a sunny day.

My family went on a picnic.

"What's this?" asked my sister.

"It's a lost kitten," said my dad.

"He looks hungry," said my sister.

"Let's give some food," said my mom.

After a meal, we played with the kitten.

We named him Kitty.

We kept playing with him till late.

# Vocabulary

## Write the Words

| this | give | meal | go | picnic | sunny |

_____

_____

_____

_____

_____

_____

## Unscramble the Letters

①

t  t
k  i  e
n

②

t  l
o  s

# After Reading

## Look and Check

 ❶
a. It's a lost kitten.
b. It's a lost puppy.

 ❷
a. It was a rainy day.
b. It was a sunny day.

 ❸
a. Let's give some food.
b. Let's make some food.

## Number the Sentences

 ❶    ❷    ❸

a. We played with the kitten. _____

b. My family went on a picnic. _____

c. We named the cat Kitty. _____

# Choose the Correct Words

1 My family _____ on a picnic.

      a. went               b. wanted

2 It's a _____ kitten.

      a. fat               b. lost

3 _____ a meal, we played with the kitten.

      a. Before          b. After

# Check True or False

1 We kept playing with the kitten till late.

      T ☐              F ☐

2 The kitten looks very hungry.

      T ☐              F ☐

3 It was a very rainy day.

      T ☐              F ☐

## Story Comprehension

1 What's the main idea?

   a. The lost baby

   b. The lost kitten

   c. The lost puppy


2 Who found the lost kitten?

   a. Mom          b. Dad          c. sister


3 What did they name the kitten?

   a. Happy        b. Kitty         c. Sally


4 How long did they play with the kitten?

   a. until noon    b. till evening    c. till late


5 What is true?

   a. The girl's family went to the river.

   b. The girl's family saw a lost puppy.

   c. The girl's family gave the kitten some food.

## Before Reading

# New Words

family

people

amusement park

viking ship

bumper car

roller-coaster

ride

wait

excited

# Key Expression

I rode on a horse.

❶ I _____ _____ a viking ship.

❷ He _____ _____ a bumper car.

# I rode on the viking ship.

My family went to the amusement park.

There were a lot of rides.

A viking ship, a bumper car and a roller-coaster....

I wanted to ride on the viking ship.

But, there were lots of people.

So we had to wait for a long time.

At last, I rode on the viking ship.

I was very excited.

We had a wonderful time.

## Vocabulary

## Write the Words

| ride | wait | excited | amusement park | bumper car | viking ship |

①

②

③

④

⑤

⑥

## Unscramble the Letters

❶

| a | f |
| i | l |
| m | y |

❷

| | o |
| p | p |
| e | l | e |

## After Reading

# Look and Check

a. My family went to the mountain.

b. My family went to the amusement park.

a. There were a lot of rides.

b. There were lots of people.

a. I wanted to ride on the viking ship.

b. I wanted to ride on the bumper car.

# Number the Sentences

a. There were people. _____

b. We had to wait for a long time. _____

c. I was very excited. _____

# Choose the Correct Words

**1** My _____ went to the amusement park.

   a. family               b. friends

**2** There were _____ rides.

   a. two                  b. a lot of

**3** We had a _____ time.

   a. terrible             b. wonderful

# Check True or False

**1** I rode on the bumper car.

   T ☐               F ☐

**2** I waited for a long time to ride the viking ship.

   T ☐               F ☐

**3** I was very tired.

   T ☐               F ☐

## Story Comprehension

1. What's the main idea?

   a. Terrible day

   b. A lot of rides

   c. Going to the amusement park

2. Where did the boy's family go?

   a. park

   b. mountain

   c. amusement park

3. Were there a lot of rides?

   a. Yes, there were.      b. No, there weren't.

4. What did the boy want to ride on?

   a. the plane

   b. the viking ship

   c. the bumper car

5. How did the boy feel?

   a. glad          b. sad          c. excited

## Before Reading

## New Words

best friend

together

every day

quarrel

shout

unhappy

sleep

night

## Key Expression

We were unhappy.

① I _____ _____ . (happy)

② They _____ _____ . (sad)

# I'm sorry.

Paul is my best friend.

Paul and I play together every day.

But yesterday, we quarreled.

I shouted at him.

He shouted back to me.

We were unhappy.

I couldn't sleep well.

Today, I said to him, "I'm sorry."

And he said to me, "I'm sorry, too."

We played together again.

We are happy now.

# Vocabulary

## Write the Words

| every day | best friend | together | sleep | night | quarrel |

1.

2.

3.

4.

5.

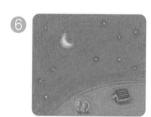

6.

## Unscramble the Letters

1. s h o t u

2. a n h p y u p

## After Reading

# Look and Check

a. Paul and I sing together.

b. Paul and I play together.

a. I smiled to him.

b. I shouted at him.

a. I said to him, "I'm sorry."

b. I said to him, "I'm okay."

# Number the Sentences

a. Paul is my best friend. _____

b. We quarreled. _____

c. We are happy now. _____

## Choose the Correct Words

1 Paul is my _____ friend.

    a. best                b. better

2 He _____ back to me.

    a. shout             b. shouted

3 We played _____ again.

    a. with               b. together

## Check True or False

1 Paul is my brother.

    T ☐            F ☐

2 Paul and I seldom play together.

    T ☐            F ☐

3 We play together again.

    T ☐            F ☐

## Story Comprehension

① What's the main idea?

   a. My friend, Paul.

   b. Singing with friends.

   c. Studying with friends.

② How often does the boy play with Paul?

   a. seldom      b. sometimes     c. every day

③ When did they quarrel?

   a. a few days ago

   b. yesterday

   c. today

④ How did they feel after quarrel?

   a. glad        b. happy       c. unhappy

⑤ What did the boy say to Paul?

   a. I'm sorry.     b. Thank you.   c. You're welcome.

## Before Reading

# New Words

brother

sister

dinner

song

read

sky

star

alone

# Key Expression

There were **a lot of stars.**

1. _____ _____ lots of animals.

2. _____ _____ books on the sofa.

## Story

# I looked up the sky.

My family has five members.
Dad, Mom, an older brother, a younger sister
and myself.
Today, we had dinner early.
I wanted to play with brother.
But Mom sang a song with my brother.
And Dad read books for my sister.
I was alone.
So I went out.
I looked up the sky.
There were a lot of stars.
I wasn't alone.

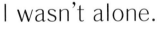

## Vocabulary

## Write the Words

dinner    alone    brother    song    read    star

①

②

③

_____

_____

_____

④

⑤

⑥

_____

_____

_____

## Unscramble the Letters

❶

i
t    s
s    e    r

_____

❷

y    s
k

_____

## After Reading

# Look and Check

 ①

    a. Mom danced with my brother.

    b. Mom sang a song with my brother.

②

    a. Dad read books with my sister.

    b. Dad played games with my sister.

③

    a. The girl flew in the sky.

    b. The girl looked up the sky.

# Number the Sentences

①    ②    ③

a. We read books. _____

b. We sang a song. _____

c. There were a lot of stars. _____

# Choose the Correct Words

1 My family had _____ early.

    a. breakfast           b. dinner

2 I wanted to _____ with my brother.

    a. play              b. sleep

3 My family has _____ members.

    a. four              b. five

# Check True or False

1 Mom played the piano with my brother.

    T ☐            F ☐

2 Dad read books for my sister.

    T ☐            F ☐

3 There were a lot of stars in the sky.

    T ☐            F ☐

## Story Comprehension

**1** What's the main idea?

   a. Dinner

   b. I was alone

   c. Singing and reading

**2** How big is the girl's family?

   a. four         b. five         c. six

**3** Who sang a song with her brother?

   a. Mom        b. Dad        c. Brother

**4** Who read books for sister?

   a. Mom        b. Dad        c. Brother

**5** What did the girl want?

   a. She wanted to eat dinner late.

   b. She wanted to see the stars.

   c. She wanted to play with her brother.

## Before Reading

## New Words

house

rabbit

moon

ask

dream

rocket

land

animal

## Key Expression

It's time **for bed.**

1 _____ _____ for lunch.

2 _____ _____ to study English.

# Can I go to the moon?

There were three rabbits in the house.
Daddy Rabbit, Mommy Rabbit,
and Baby Rabbit.
"Can I go to the moon?" asked the Baby Rabbit.
"No, you can't," said the Mommy Rabbit.
"It's time for bed."
Baby Rabbit went to bed.
She dreamed.
She rode on a rocket.
And she landed on the moon.
She met lots of animals.

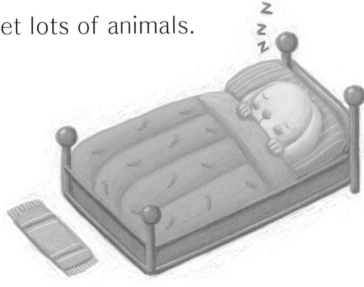

## Vocabulary

## Write the Words

rocket   rabbit   dream   animal   land   ask

①

②

③

④

⑤

⑥

## Unscramble the Letters

❶

o u
h e s

❷

o
m n
o

## After Reading

## Look and Check

a. There were four rabbits in the house.

b. There were three rabbits in the house.

a. Baby Rabbit got up.

b. Baby Rabbit went to bed.

a. Baby Rabbit rode on a plane.

b. Baby Rabbit rode on a rocket.

## Number the Sentences

a. Baby Rabbit landed on the moon. _____

b. Baby Rabbit met lots of animals. _____

c. There were three rabbits. _____

# Choose the Correct Words

➊ It's _____ for bed.

      a. time            b. clock

➋ Baby Rabbit _____ lots of animals.

      a. met            b. went

➌ Baby Rabbit _____ on the moon.

      a. left            b. landed

# Check True or False

➊ "Can I go to the moon?" asked the Baby Rabbit.

      T ☐            F ☐

➋ Baby Rabbit didn't go to bed.

      T ☐            F ☐

➌ Baby Rabbit dreamed.

      T ☐            F ☐

## Story Comprehension

① What's the main idea?

   a. Moon

   b. Baby rabbit's rocket

   c. Baby rabbit's dream

② How many rabbits were there in the house?

   a. two          b. three         c. four

③ What did the Baby Rabbit ride on?

   a. a bus         b. a bike        c. a rocket

④ Where did the Baby Rabbit land on?

   a. the sea       b. the moom      c. the earth

⑤ Baby Rabbit met lots of _____ on the moon.

   a. people       b. angels       c. animals

## Before Reading

# New Words

fish

river

swim

here

deep

climb

tree

high

fun

# Key Expression

Jack learned how to fish.

1 I learned _____ _____ play the guitar.

2 They learned _____ _____ ride skates.

**Story**

## I want to swim.

Dad and Jack went to the river.

Dad wanted to fish with Jack.

But Jack didn't want to fish.

Jack said, "I want to swim."

Dad said, "Not here, too deep."

Jack said, "I want to climb up that tree."

Dad said, "Not that tree, too high."

Jack said, "I see, Dad."

Jack learned how to fish.

It was a lot of fun.

Dad and Jack had a wonderful time.

## Vocabulary

# Write the Words

| here | fish | river | tree | high | deep |

① _____

② _____

③ _____

④ _____

⑤ _____

⑥ _____

# Unscramble the Letters

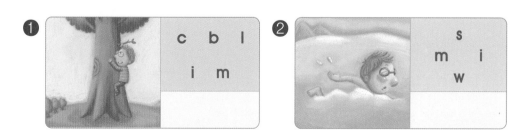

① c b l
i m

② s
m i
w

# After Reading

## Look and Check

**1**

a. Dad and Jack went to the river.

b. Dad and Jack went to the mountain.

**2**

a. Jack learned how to fish.

b. Jack learned how to swim.

**3**

a. Dad and Jack were fishing in the river.

b. Dad and Jack were climbing up the tree.

## Number the Sentences

a. The river is very deep. _____

b. The tree is very high. _____

c. Jack said, "I want to swim." _____

# Choose the Correct Words

1 Dad said, "Not here, too _____."

    a. shallow        b. deep

2 He learned _____ fish.

    a. how to        b. where to

3 Jack said, "I want to climb _____ that tree."

    a. up        b. under

# Check True or False

1 Dad and Jack went to the river.

    T ☐        F ☐

2 Dad said, "Not that tree, too high."

    T ☐        F ☐

3 Jack said, "I want to fish."

    T ☐        F ☐

## Story Comprehension

1. What is the main idea?

   a. Fishing

   b. Camping

   c. Swimming

2. Where did Jack and Dad go?

   a. sea           b. river           c. field

3. What did Jack want to do?

   a. swimming and fishing

   b. fishing and climbing up the tree

   c. swimming and climbing up the tree

4. Dad said, "Not that tree, too _____."

   a. deep          b. high          c. short

5. Dad said, "Not here, too _____."

   a. deep          b. thin          c. shallow

## Before Reading

## New Words

dinosaur

expo(exposition)

home

kid

tired

back

fly

neck

## Key Expression

Many kids liked to play them.

❶ I _____ _____ drink some milk.

❷ We _____ _____ play basketball.

Unit 20 **123**

# Dinosaurs came back.

Sam went to a dinosaur expo with his family.

And he came home late.

So he was very tired.

He fell asleep soon and dreamed.

Dinosaurs came back.

Many kids played with dinosaurs.

Some kids rode on a dinosaur's back.

Other kids ran with dinosaurs.

Other kids flied on a dinosaur's neck.

Dinosaurs and kids all looked happy.

# Vocabulary

## Write the Words

| kid   back   tired   fly   neck   dinosaur |

1

2

3

4

5

6

## Unscramble the Letters

1

x
o    p
e

2

o
h    e
m

## After Reading

## Look and Check

1
    a. He came back early.
    b. He came back late.

2
    a. He went to animals expo.
    b. He went to a dinosaur expo.

3
    a. Some kids rode on a dinosaur's tail.
    b. Some kids rode on a dinosaur's back.

## Number the Sentences

a. He fell asleep and dreamed. _____

b. He was very tired. _____

c. Other kids ran with a dinosaur. _____

# Choose the Correct Words

**1** He came home _____ .

    a. late            b. lately

**2** Dinosaurs came _____ .

    a. back           b. home

**3** He fell _____ and dreamed.

    a. sleep          b. asleep

# Check True or False

**1** He went to a dinosaur expo with his friends.

    T ☐           F ☐

**2** He was very scared.

    T ☐           F ☐

**3** Some kids rode on a dinosaur's back.

    T ☐           F ☐

## Story Comprehension

① What's the main idea?

   a. Sam's family

   b. Sam's dream

   c. A dinosaur expo

② Where did the boy go with his family?

   a. A bird expo

   b. A book expo

   c. A dinosaur expo

③ When did his family come back home?

   a. early in the morning

   b. at noon

   c. late at night

④ What did he dream about?

   a. about an expo

   b. about his family

   c. about kids and dinosaurs

⑤ What is not true?

   a. Some kids rode on a dinosaur's back.

   b. Other kids flied on a dinosaur's neck.

   c. Other kids swam with dinosaurs.

# 스토리 해석 및 정답

### Story        10p

**새끼돼지는 어디 있죠?**

농장에 아기 동물들이 있어요.
아기 돼지는 어디 있죠?
진흙탕 속에 있어요.
아기 양은 어디 있죠?
진흙탕 주위에 있네요.
아기 오리는 어디 있죠?
울타리 위에 있네요.
송아지는 어디 있죠?
울타리 뒤에 있네요.

### Vocabulary        11p

Write the Words

1 lamb    2 calf    3 in
4 by    5 piglet    6 fence

Unscramble the Letters

1 mud    2 behind

### After Reading        12~13p

Look and Check

1 a    2 a    3 a

Number the Sentences

a. 3    b. 2    c. 1

Choose the Correct Words

1 b    2 b    3 a

Check True or False

1 T    2 F    3 F

### Story Comprehension        14p

1 c    2 a    3 b
4 a    5 b

## Unit 2

### Story        16p

**하지 마, 짐.**

나는 남동생이 있어요.
그의 이름은 짐이에요.
그는 장난꾸러기 소년이에요.
그는 꽃병을 깨요.
엄마가 말해요. "하지 마, 짐."
그는 책을 던져요.
아빠가 말해요. "하지 마, 짐."
그는 개의 꼬리를 잡아당겨요.
우리 가족은 모두 그에게 말해요
"하지 마, 짐."

## Vocabulary                                    17p

### Write the Words

1 tail    2 pull    3 naughty
4 book    5 throw   6 younger

### Unscramble the Letters

1 vase    2 break

## After Reading                           18~19p

### Look and Check

1 a    2 b    3 a

### Number the Sentences

a. 2    b. 3    c. 1

### Choose the Correct Words

1 a    2 b    3 b

### Check True or False

1 F    2 F    3 T

## Story Comprehension                      20p

1 c    2 c    3 Jim
4 c    5 a

## Unit 3

### Key Expression                            21p

1 am looking for
2 is looking for

## Story                                        22p

### 세 마리의 쥐

세 마리의 쥐가 있어요.
세 마리의 쥐는 배가 고파요.
그리고 졸리기도 해요.
그들은 음식을 찾고 있어요.
그들은 계단을 올라가요.
드디어, 그들은 3층에서 치즈를 발견해요.
그리고 침대도 3개가 있어요.
그들은 치즈를 먹어요.
그들은 이제 배가 불러요.
세 마리의 쥐는 이제 침대로 가고 싶어요.

## Vocabulary                                    23p

### Write the Words

1 mice    2 climb    3 hungry
4 cheese  5 find     6 stairs

### Unscramble the Letters

1 sleepy    2 food

## After Reading                           24~25p

### Look and Check

1 b    2 b    3 a

### Number the Sentences

a. 2    b. 1    c. 3

### Choose the Correct Words

1 b    2 b    3 b

Check True or False
① F     ② F     ③ T

 Story Comprehension          26p

① c     ② a     ③ c
④ c     ⑤ c


## Unit 4

Key Expression                27p
① ② learn to

Story                         28p

**나는 많은 것을 배워요.**

나는 동물들로부터 많은 것을 배워요.
나는 개에게서 달리는 것을 배워요.
나는 고양이에게서 점프하는 것을 배워요.
나는 새에게서 노래하는 것을 배워요.
나는 동물들과 함께 행복해요.

그리고 나는 사람들로부터 많은 것을 배워요.
나는 아빠에게서 책을 읽는 것을 배워요.
나는 선생님에게서 공부하는 것을 배워요.
나는 친구들에게서 노는 것을 배워요.
나는 사람들과 함께 행복해요.


Vocabulary                    29p

Write the Words

① study    ② teacher    ③ run
④ sing     ⑤ jump

Unscramble the Letters
① friend   ② play

After Reading                 30~31p

Look and Check
① b        ② a          ③ b

Number the Sentences
a. ②       b. ③         c. ①

Choose the Correct Words
① a        ② b          ③ b

Check True or False
① T        ② F          ③ T

Story Comprehension           32p

① b        ② a          ③ b
④ c        ⑤ c


## Unit 5

Key Expression                33p
① was born    ② were born

**Story**      34p

### 그들은 좋은 친구들이에요.

많은 어린이들이 있어요.
주디는 말랐어요.
제이크는 시각 장애인이에요.
애니는 뚱뚱해요.
신디는 청각 장애인이에요.
에릭은 키가 커요.
피터는 키가 작아요.
그들은 조금 다르게 태어났어요.
그들은 하느님의 눈에는 모두 같아요.
그들은 좋은 친구들이에요.

**Vocabulary**      35p

**Write the Words**

① same    ② fat    ③ thin
④ blind    ⑤ short    ⑥ tall

**Unscramble the Letters**
① children    ② deaf

**After Reading**      36~37p

**Look and Check**

① b      ② a      ③ b

**Number the Sentences**
a. ②      b. ①      c. ③

**Choose the Correct Words**
① b      ② b      ③ b

**Check True or False**
① T      ② F      ③ T

**Story Comprehension**      38p

① b      ② Eric      ③ Cindy
④ Peter      ⑤ Jake

## Unit 6

**Key Expression**      39p
① am cleaning    ② are playing

**Story**      40p

### 아기가 언제 나와요?

우리는 새 아기를 갖게 될 거예요.
아빠는 요람을 만들고 있어요.
엄마는 아기의 옷을 만들고 있어요.
누나는 거실을 청소하고 있어요.
나는 아기의 욕조를 닦고 있어요.
"아기가 언제 나와요?"
나는 엄마에게 물어요.
엄마는 대답해요. "곧."
나는 아기에게 내 곰인형을 줄 거예요.
나는 아기에게 내 로봇도 줄 거예요.

**Vocabulary**      41p

**Write the Words**

① teddy bear      ② living room

③ clothes        ④ bathtub
⑤ clean          ⑥ new

## Unscramble the Letters
① cradle         ② robot

### After Reading                42~43p

## Look and Check
① b          ② b          ③ b

## Number the Sentences
a. ②        b. ③        c. ①

## Choose the Correct Words
① b          ② b          ③ a

## Check True or False
① F          ② F          ③ T

### Story Comprehension          44p

① c          ② a          ③ c
④ c          ⑤ c


## Unit 7

### Key Expression              45p
① dog's
② duck's

### Story                        46p

## 그들은 너무 귀여워요!
닭 한 마리와 오리 한 마리가 있어요.
닭은 자기의 알 위에 앉아 있어요.
오리도 자기의 알 위에 앉아 있어요.
닭의 알이 부화해요.
오리의 알도 부화해요.
닭은 말해요. "내 어린 아기야!"
오리는 말해요. "내 어린 아기야!"
병아리와 새끼오리는 걷고 있어요.
그들은 너무 귀여워요!

### Vocabulary                   47p

## Write the Words
① egg       ② hen       ③ chick
④ duck      ⑤ hatch     ⑥ duckling

## Unscramble the Letters
① little     ② walk

### After Reading                48~49p

## Look and Check
① a          ② a          ③ a

## Number the Sentences
a. ②        b. ③        c. ①

## Choose the Correct Words
① a          ② b          ③ b

## Check True or False

① T ② F ③ F

**Story Comprehension** 50p

① c ② a ③ c
④ c ⑤ a

## Unit 8

### Key Expression 51p
① her ② him

**Story** 52p

**나는 너무 슬퍼요.**

우리 식구들은 모두 나를 좋아했어요.
엄마와 아빠는 나를 좋아했어요.
할머니와 할아버지도 나를 좋아했어요.
하지만 더 이상 아무도 나를 좋아하지
않아요.
왜냐하면 여동생이 태어났기 때문이에요.
나는 내 여동생이 싫어요.
그래서 나는 내 여동생의 팔을 꼬집
었어요.
엄마와 아빠는 나에게 화를 냈어요.
할머니와 할아버지는 나를 꾸짖었고요.
나는 너무 슬퍼요.

**Vocabulary** 53p

### Write the Words

① pinch ② like ③ grandpa
④ grandma ⑤ arm ⑥ sad

### Unscramble the Letters
① hate ② scold

**After Reading** 54~55p

### Look and Check
① b ② b ③ a

### Number the Sentences
a. ③ b. ① c. ②

### Choose the Correct Words
① a ② b ③ a

### Check True or False
① T ② F ③ T

**Story Comprehension** 56p

① c ② b ③ a
④ b ⑤ c

## Unit 9

### Key Expression 57p
① has, headache
② have, toothache

**Story**      58p

**아기 하마 배 속의 장난감들**

엄마 하마가 말해요. "의사선생님, 의사
선생님, 우리 아기가 아파요."
의사선생님이 말해요. "어디가 아프니?"
아기 하마는 말해요. "배가 아파요."
의사가 말해요. "좀 보도록 하자...
아, 너의 배 속에 장난감들이 들어 있구나."
의사선생님은 장난감을 꺼내요.
자동차 1개, 트럭 1개, 그리고 보트 1개.
의사선생님이 말해요. "이제 괜찮니?"
아기 하마는 말해요.
"훨씬 좋아졌어요. 고맙습니다, 의사선생님"

**Vocabulary**      59p

**Write the Words**

① car      ② stomachache
③ hippo      ④ doctor
⑤ boat      ⑥ truck

**Unscramble the Letters**

① sick      ② stomach

**After Reading**      60~61p

**Look and Check**

① b      ② b      ③ a

**Number the Sentences**

a. ③      b. ①      c. ②

**Choose the Correct Words**

① a      ② b      ③ b

**Check True or False**

① F      ② T      ③ T

**Story Comprehension**      62p

① b      ② c      ③ a
④ a      ⑤ a

## Unit 10

**Key Expression**      63p

① sometimes      ② never

**Story**      64p

**신디의 나쁜 습관**

신디는 예쁜 소녀예요.
그리고 수줍은 소녀예요.
그녀는 나쁜 습관이 있었어요.
그녀는 종종 그녀의 손톱을 깨물어요.
그녀는 때때로 그녀의 코를 후벼요.
그녀가 손톱을 깨물 때마다 엄마는
말해요. "그렇게 하지 마!"
그녀가 코를 후빌 때마다
아빠는 말해요. "그렇게 하지 마."
이제, 신디는 절대로 손톱을 깨물지 않아요.
그녀는 결코 그녀의 코를 후비지 않아요.

## Vocabulary 65p

### Write the Words
① bite ② nose ③ girl
④ nail ⑤ pretty

### Unscramble the Letters
① pick ② shy

## After Reading 66~67p

### Look and Check
① b ② a ③ b

### Number the Sentences
a. ③ b. ① c. ②

### Choose the Correct Words
① b ② b ③ b

### Check True or False
① F ② F ③ T

## Story Comprehension 68p

① c ② c ③ b
④ a ⑤ c

## Unit 11

### Key Expression 69p
① are, doing ② is, going

## Story 70p

### 너와 함께 가도 되니?

더운 여름날이에요.
숲 속에 물이 하나도 없어요.
여우는 목이 말랐어요.
그래서 여우는 물을 찾기 위해서 숲을
떠나요.
여우는 가는 길에 까마귀를 만나요.
까마귀는 여우에게 말해요.
"너는 어디에 가는 중이니?"
여우는 말해요.
"나는 물을 찾기 위해서 가고 있어."
"나도 너와 함께 가도 될까?"
까마귀가 말해요.
"물론이야!" 여우가 말해요.
그래서 그들은 함께 물을 찾으러 가요.

## Vocabulary 71p

### Write the Words
① summer ② thirsty
③ crow ④ woods
⑤ fox ⑥ hot

### Unscramble the Letters
① water ② meet

## After Reading 72~73p

### Look and Check
① a ② a ③ a

Number the Sentences

a. ❶        b. ❸        c. ❷

Choose the Correct Words

❶ b        ❷ b        ❸ a

Check True or False

❶ F        ❷ F        ❸ T

 **Story Comprehension**        74p

❶ c        ❷ b        ❸ c
❹ c        ❺ a

## Unit 12

Key Expression        75p
❶ am good at        ❷ are good at

**Story**        76p

### 주디는 요리하는 것을 좋아해요.

사람들은 먹는 것을 좋아해요.
하지만 주디는 요리하는 것을 좋아해요.
그녀는 요리를 잘해요.
그래서 그녀는 훌륭한 주방장이 되기를 원해요.
때때로 그녀는 가족을 위해서 음식을 만들었어요.
그녀는 엄마를 위해서 샌드위치를 만들었어요.
그녀는 아빠를 위해서 핫도그를 만들었어요.
그녀는 남동생을 위해서 핫케이크를 만들었어요.

그녀는 자신을 위해 스크램블드 에그를 만들었어요.
그것들은 모두 맛있었어요.
다음에, 주디는 케이크를 구워 볼 거예요.

**Vocabulary**        77p

Write the Words

❶ hot dog        ❷ scrambled egg
❸ sandwiches    ❹ cook
❺ hot cakes     ❻ cake

Unscramble the Letters
❶ chef          ❷ delicious

**After Reading**        78~79p

Look and Check

❶ b        ❷ a        ❸ a

Number the Sentences

a. ❶        b. ❸        c. ❷

Choose the Correct Words

❶ b        ❷ b        ❸ a

Check True or False

❶ T        ❷ T        ❸ F

**Story Comprehension**        80p

❶ b        ❷ c        ❸ c
❹ b        ❺ c

## Unit 13

### Key Expression          81p
① ② Let's

 **Story**          82p

**제이크는 어린이용 의자가 있어요.**

제이크는 어린이용 의자가 있어요.
그 의자는 파란색이에요.
그는 그 의자에 앉아서 음식을 먹었어요.
어느날 아빠가 그에게 말했어요.
"그 의자를 분홍색으로 칠하자."
제이크는 물었어요, "왜요, 아빠?"
아빠는 대답했어요. "너의 여동생을 위해서."
제이크는 생각하고 대답했어요.
"알았어요, 아빠."
그들은 의자를 분홍색으로 칠했어요.

 **Vocabulary**          83p

**Write the Words**

① high chair      ② paint
③ pink            ④ eat
⑤ blue            ⑥ say

**Unscramble the Letters**

① sit             ② think

**After Reading**          84~85p

**Look and Check**

① b      ② a      ③ b

**Number the Sentences**

a. ②          b. ①          c. ③

**Choose the Correct Words**

① b          ② b          ③ b

**Check True or False**

① T          ② F          ③ F

 **Story Comprehension**          86p

① c          ② b          ③ a
④ a          ⑤ a

## Unit 14

### Key Expression          87p
① ② went on

**Story**          88p

**우리는 그 고양이에게 키티라는 이름을 지어주었어요.**

화창한 날이었어요.
우리 가족은 소풍을 갔어요.
"이것이 뭐예요?" 여동생이 물었어요.
"길 잃은 새끼 고양이구나." 아빠가 말했어요.
"배가 고파 보여요." 여동생이 말했어요.
"음식을 좀 주는 게 좋겠다." 엄마가 말했어요.
식사 후에, 우리는 고양이와 함께 놀았어요.

우리는 그 고양이에게 키티라는 이름을
지어주었어요.
우리는 늦게까지 놀았어요.

### Vocabulary
89p
## Write the Words

1 give    2 sunny
3 meal    4 go
5 this    6 picnic

## Unscramble the Letters
1 kitten    2 lost

### After Reading
90~91p

## Look and Check
1 a    2 b    3 a

## Number the Sentences
a. 1    b. 2    c. 3

## Choose the Correct Words
1 a    2 b    3 b

## Check True or False
1 T    2 T    3 F

### Story Comprehension
92p

1 b    2 c    3 b
4 c    5 c

## Unit 15

### Key Expression
93p
1 2 rode on

### Story
94p

## 바이킹을 탔어요.

우리 가족은 놀이공원에 갔어요.
수많은 다양한 놀이기구가 있었어요.
바이킹, 범퍼카, 그리고 롤러코스터...
나는 바이킹을 타고 싶었어요.
하지만 사람들이 많았어요.
그래서 우리는 오랫동안 기다려야만 했어요.
드디어 나는 바이킹을 탔어요.
정말 재미있었어요.
우리는 멋진 시간을 보냈어요.

### Vocabulary
95p
## Write the Words

1 ride        2 bumper car
3 wait        4 viking ship
5 excited     6 amusement park

## Unscramble the Letters
1 family    2 people

### After Reading
96~97p
## Look and Check

1 b    2 a    3 a

## Number the Sentences
a. ②      b. ③      c. ①

## Choose the Correct Words
① a      ② b      ③ b

## Check True or False
① F      ② T      ③ F

 **Story Comprehension**     98p

① c      ② c      ③ a
④ b      ⑤ c

## Unit 16

### Key Expression     99p
① was happy    ② were sad

**Story**     100p

**미안해.**

폴은 내 가장 친한 친구예요.
폴과 나는 매일 함께 놀아요.
그러나 어제 우리는 다퉜어요.
나는 그에게 소리를 질렀어요.
그도 나에게 소리를 질렀어요.
우리는 기분이 좋지 않았어요.
나는 밤에 잠을 잘 자지 못했어요.
오늘, 나는 그에게 "미안해."라고 말했
어요.

그리고 그도 나에게, "나도 미안해."라
고 말했어요.
우리는 다시 함께 놀았어요.
우리는 지금 행복해요.

**Vocabulary**     101p

## Write the Words
① quarrel    ② sleep
③ together    ④ every day
⑤ best friend    ⑥ night

## Unscramble the Letters
① shout    ② unhappy

**After Reading**     102~103p

## Look and Check
① b      ② b      ③ a

## Number the Sentences
a. ②      b. ①      c. ③

## Choose the Correct Words
① a      ② b      ③ b

## Check True or False
① F      ② F      ③ T

**Story Comprehension**     104p

① a      ② c      ③ b
④ c      ⑤ a

아기 토끼는 침대로 갔어요.
아기 토끼는 꿈을 꿨어요.
아기 토끼는 로켓을 탔어요.
그리고 달나라에 도착했어요.
아기 토끼는 많은 동물을 만났어요.

**Vocabulary**                    113p

## Write the Words

1 rocket          2 ask
3 land            4 animal
5 dream           6 rabbit

## Unscramble the Letters

1 house           2 moon

**After Reading**          114~115p

## Look and Check

1 b          2 b          3 b

## Number the Sentences

a. 3          b. 1          c. 2

## Choose the Correct Words

1 a          2 a          3 b

## Check True or False

1 T          2 F          3 T

**Story Comprehension**        116p

1 c          2 b          3 c
4 b          5 c

## Unit 19

## Key Expression                    117p

1 2 how to

**Story**                          118p

## 나는 수영하고 싶어요.

아빠와 잭은 강에 갔어요.
아빠는 잭과 함께 낚시를 하고 싶었어요.
하지만 잭은 낚시가 하고 싶지 않았어요.
잭은 말해요. "저는 수영하고 싶어요."
아빠는 말해요.
"여기서는 안 돼. 너무 깊어."
잭은 말해요.
"저는 저 나무에 올라가고 싶어요."
아빠가 말해요. "저 나무는 안 돼, 너무 높아."
잭은 말해요. "알았어요, 아빠."
잭은 낚시하는 법을 배워요.
낚시는 정말 재미있었어요.
아빠와 잭은 멋진 시간을 보냈어요.

**Vocabulary**                    119p

## Write the Words

1 high           2 here
3 deep           4 river
5 fish           6 swim

## Unscramble the Letters

1 climb          2 swim

## After Reading　　　120~121p

### Look and Check
① a　　　② a　　　③ a

### Number the Sentences
a. ①　　　b. ③　　　c. ②

### Choose the Correct Words
① b　　　② a　　　③ a

### Check True or False
① T　　　② T　　　③ F

## Story Comprehension　　122p
① a　　　② b　　　③ c
④ b　　　⑤ a

## Unit 20

### Key Expression　　123p
① ② liked to

## Story　　124p

**공룡이 돌아왔다.**

샘은 그의 가족과 함께 '공룡전시회'를 갔다.
그리고 집에 늦게 돌아왔다.
그래서 샘은 매우 피곤했다.
그는 곧 잠이 들었고 꿈을 꾸었다.
공룡이 돌아왔다.

많은 아이들이 공룡들과 함께 놀았다.
어떤 아이들은 공룡의 등을 올라탔다.
어떤 아이들은 공룡과 함께 달렸다.
어떤 아이들은 공룡의 목을 타고 날았다.
공룡들과 아이들은 모두 행복해 보였다.

## Vocabulary　　125p

### Write the Words
① dinosaur ② kid ③ back
④ neck ⑤ fly ⑥ tired

### Unscramble the Letters
① expo　② home

## After Reading　　126~127p

### Look and Check
① b　　　② b　　　③ b

### Number the Sentences
a. ②　　　b. ①　　　c. ③

### Choose the Correct Words
① a　　　② a　　　③ b

### Check True or False
① F　　　② F　　　③ T

## Story Comprehension　　128p
① b　　　② c　　　③ c
④ c　　　⑤ c